Hernando de Soto

Ruth Manning

DATE DUE

Heinemann Library
Chicago, Illinois

©2001 Reed Educational & Professional Publishing
Published by Heinemann Library,
an imprint of Reed Educational & Professional Publishing,
Chicago, IL

Customer Service 888-454-2279

Visit our website at www.heinemannlibrary.com

Designed by Wilkinson Design
Illustrated by Art
Printed by Wing King Tong, in Hong Kong

05 04 03
10 9 8 7 6 5 4 3 2

Library of Congress Cataloging-in-Publication Data
Manning, Ruth.
    Hernando de Soto / Ruth Manning.
        p. cm. – (Groundbreakers)
    Includes bibliographical references (p.) and index.
    Summary: A biography of the wealthy Spanish explorer who became the first white man to cross the Mississippi.
    ISBN 1-57572-388-3 (lib. bdg.)   ISBN 1-58810-343-9 (pbk. bdg.)
        1. Soto, Hernando de, ca. 1500-1542—Juvenile literature. 2.
Explorers—America—Biography—Juvenile literature. 3.
Explorers—Spain—Biography—Juvenile literature. 4. America—Discovery and exploration—Spanish—Juvenile literature. 5. Southern States—Discovery and exploration—Spanish—Juvenile literature. [1. De Soto, Hernando, ca. 1500-1542. 2.
Explorers.] I. Title. II. Series.

E125.S7 .F67 2000
970.01'6'092—dc21
[B]   00-029573

Acknowledgments The publisher would like to thank the following for permission to reproduce photographs:
North Wind, pp. 4, 7 (center), 8, 14, 19, 21, 23, 25, 26, 27, 29, 33, 34, 37, 38; The Granger Collection, pp. 5, 20, 22; Stock Montage, pp. 7 (bottom), 11; Galleria Borghese, Rome/The Bridgeman Art Library, p. 9; Private Collection/The Bridgeman Art Library, p.10; Corbis, pp. 12, 13, 39, 40; Pedro Martinez/South American Pictures, p. 15; Mary Evans Picture Library, pp. 16, 18, 24; New York Public Library, p. 17; Florida Division of Historical Resources, p. 28; John Nees/Earth Scenes, p. 30; Library of Congress, pp. 31, 36; The Library of Congress Collection /The Bridgeman Art Library, p. 32; John Berkey/National Geographic Image Collection, p. 35.

Cover photograph: The Granger Collection

Some words are shown in bold, **like this.**
You can find out what they mean by looking in the glossary.

Contents

Explorer of the Americas

Achievements in North America

When Hernando de Soto crossed the wide Mississippi River in 1541, it was a great moment in a life filled with triumphs. As the leader of an expedition authorized by the Spanish king, de Soto had explored territory in what is now Florida, Georgia, South Carolina, North Carolina, Tennessee, Alabama, Mississippi, Arkansas, and Louisiana. Except for Florida, members of de Soto's party were the first Europeans to enter these lands.

He came as a Spanish **conquistador**—a soldier who claimed territory for his king and who brought his Christian faith with him. Sometimes he was received in peace. Sometimes he faced hostile forces from Native Americans. On his trek through North America, he did not find any of the fabulous gold of Mexico or Peru. Instead, he found good farmland that was rich in other resources. More important to him, he made his own discovery—finding the Mississippi River. He had seen other Spanish conquistadors like Balboa find the Pacific Ocean and Pizarro contact and conquer the **Incas.**

De Soto discovered more territory traveling over land routes than any other explorer of his day.

Central and South America

De Soto had already made a name and a fortune for himself in Panama and Nicaragua. He lent Pizarro two ships for his exploration off the coast of South America and joined Pizarro's expedition as one of its chief leaders, captain of the horse. He was known as one of the finest horsemen and fighters with the **lance.** De Soto was the first European to make contact with the Inca **emperor,** Atahualpa. He took part in the battle at Cajamarca, at which the Spaniards conquered the Incas against great odds. He went on to seize Cuzco, the Inca capital. After receiving his share of the Incas' gold, he left Peru as one of the wealthiest conquistadors who returned to Spain.

In his homeland, the king honored de Soto. He asked the king for permission to conquer Ecuador and gain rights to the Amazon River basin. Instead, he was told to conquer Florida and was made governor of Cuba, with his own command of forces. Then, in 1539, he began his exploration of what is now the southeastern United States.

De Soto is best known for his discovery of the Mississippi River in May of 1541.

Second Son

De Soto's family

De Soto's exact date of birth is not known. Most historians put it between 1496 and 1501. He was born to a **noble** family in Jerez de los Caballeros in Spain. Unfortunately, he was the second son. According to tradition, the first son inherited all of the property and the family name. In this way, a family's wealth could be kept together without splitting it among many children. Thus it was Juan, the oldest son, who was given the property, the name of Mendez de Soto—while Hernando was just de Soto—and the responsibility of caring for his sisters.

Hernando, however, was his mother's favorite. She hoped that he would grow up to be a lawyer or even a priest. Thus, he was given the best education the family could provide. However, Hernando had other ideas. He was tall, strong, and adventurous. When he was fourteen, he looked much older. He wanted to join the Spanish soldiers who were fighting in Italy. His father wanted him to continue his studies, but his local teacher was not encouraging. Because the family had financial problems, his father thought that the best option was to send Hernando off to fight. That way, Hernando would be able to earn a living without support from his family.

0 100 200 miles	
0 200 km	

Bay of Biscay

FRANCE

GALICIA

Leon

LEON
Valladolid

CATALONIA

Barcelona

Salamanca

ARAGON

EXTREMADURA

Madrid

PORTUGAL
CASTILE
Toledo

Palma

SPAIN
Valencia

BALEARIC
ISLANDS

Lisbon

Jerez de los Caballeros

Cordoba

ANADALUCIA
GRANADA

*Mediterranean
Sea*

Seville

Malaga

Cadiz

Tangier   Gibraltar

*Atlantic
Ocean*

Oran

This map shows Spain in the 16th century and the birthplace of de Soto.

Life in Spain

The town where de Soto was born was named after the **Knights Templar,** a military order that fought in the crusades. It was in the province of Extremadura—a hard country to farm but one that produced many of the most famous **conquistadors.** Vasco Núñez de Balboa, from the very same town of Jerez de los Caballeros, had already gone to this land beyond the sea that Christopher Columbus had discovered in 1492. As a child, Hernando must have heard exciting tales of this new frontier. Other youngsters from Extremadura were inspired to seek their fortunes abroad. Later, Hernán Cortés became the conqueror of the Aztecs of Mexico, and Francisco Pizarro would take on the **Incas** of Peru.

News of this larger world reached people in Extremadura along the rivers that flowed to the coast of Portugal. How exciting it must have been for the people in Hernando's town to learn about the latest discoveries in the strange lands that were called the New World.

Balboa, who sighted the Pacific Ocean; Pizarro, who conquered the Incas in Peru; and Cortés, who conquered the Aztecs in Mexico, were among the most important of the Spanish explorers.

Spain and Exploration

A nation of soldiers

Exploring new lands required careful planning. Two of the most important resources needed were people and money. In de Soto's time, Spain had a great supply of soldiers. Two large parts of Spain had been brought together with the marriage of Isabella of Castile and Ferdinand of Aragon in 1469. They had a common enemy—the **Moors,** who had ruled in the south of Spain for years. Ferdinand and Isabella succeeded in regaining control of this territory and then fought wars in Italy. When their soldiers were not fighting in foreign wars, they were squabbling over land at home.

In 1493, Christopher Columbus returned to the **court** of Isabella and Ferdinand with news of lands beyond the Atlantic Ocean. The possibility of quick routes to the riches of India could not have come at a better time. The unemployed soldiers now had new ways of gaining riches. The queen and king had a way to gain new land. The Roman Catholic Church had a new opportunity to spread Christianity. The **pope** divided the New World between Spain and Portugal and blessed the efforts of these nations to settle in the new land.

After securing control of all of Spain, Ferdinand and Isabella turned their attention to the possibilities of the New World.

The Holy Roman Empire

In 1516, after the death of Isabella and Ferdinand, their grandson, a young sixteen-year-old, came to the throne of Spain as Charles I. He was about the same age as de Soto and would be the monarch who most influenced the explorer's life. This king had already ruled in the Netherlands, picked up the title to Austria, and become the **emperor** of the Holy Roman Empire as Charles V in 1519. With gold flooding in from the New World, Spain was a world power— though not without challenges and demands for wealth for the wars of the European **empire.** Charles remained in power until 1556, fourteen years after de Soto's death.

Many of the tactics that seem so cruel today were once common practice in the wars of Europe. Soldiers were paid through their **plunder.** Kings and nobles were often held for **ransom.** Vicious dogs were turned loose on people. What the **conquistadors** practiced in the New World, they learned in the Old World of Europe.

Charles V became emperor of the Holy Roman Empire in 1519.

FACTS

The Holy Roman Empire
This empire was formed long after the fall of the Roman Empire. The Holy Roman emperors would like to have controlled the territory that the Romans conquered, so they used the name "Roman" for their land. The emperors also wanted to be recognized by the pope, so they added the name "Holy."

Ticket to the new World

Page to Pedrarias

Armed with a letter of recommendation from his school master, Friar Diego, de Soto made his way to Seville, the political center of his country. It was here that ships were prepared for voyages to the New World. The letter landed him a position as **page** to an important person, **Don** Pedro Arias Davila. Pedrarias, as he was known, had served in the wars of Isabella and Ferdinand. The king had appointed him governor of the territory in what is now Panama, and he led about 3,000 men in 20 ships. De Soto probably set sail with him sometime around 1514.

Along with three other pages, also from **noble** families, de Soto had household duties that brought him in daily contact with Pedrarias's wife and daughters. The wife, Doña Isabel de Bobadilla y Penalosa, was influential at the king's and queen's **court.** She took an interest in this young page and polished his manners. Her two youngest daughters—Isabel, 9, and Elvira, 7—were with her. De Soto developed close friendships with them, especially with Isabel. Most important, de Soto learned about the New World to which he was sailing and the politics and partnerships among the men on board.

YOU CAN FOLLOW DE SOTO'S VOYAGE ON THE MAP ON PAGE 43.

Seville in the 16th century was a rich and prosperous city and a center for outfitting expeditions to the New World.

Harsh lessons in the New World

One of de Soto's close friends from the trip across the sea was named Diego San Martín. When San Martín failed to return to the ship on time at one of the ports, Pedrarias ordered him to be taken ashore and hanged. De Soto saw a different, crueler side of the master he served.

De Soto lost another friend to the anger of Pedrarias. Balboa, the famous European discoverer of the Pacific Ocean, was from de Soto's hometown. When de Soto had settled in Panama, Balboa offered him **fencing** lessons. De Soto readily accepted his offer and his friendship. However, the competition for power between Pedrarias and Balboa resulted in the beheading of Balboa in 1519. He was charged with **treachery** to the king.

In 1513, Balboa became the first European to see the Pacific Ocean. Not realizing how vast it was, he claimed all the lands it touched for Spain.

De Soto first saw fighting at Panama. He was the youngest of a party of 150 men who crossed the narrow strip of land to the Pacific Ocean. They were under the leadership of Gaspar de Morales, authorized by Pedrarias. Francisco Pizarro was along on this trip, as were two men who became future business partners: Hernán Ponce de León and Francisco Campañón. The fighting was fierce. The Spaniards lost over half of their soldiers, but the use of dogs and guns spread fear among the natives. De Soto fought well. Though young—perhaps even still a teenager—he was promoted to the rank of captain of the **lancers.**

Ambitions of a Young Man

Loyalty to Pedrarias

Why did de Soto remain loyal to a man like Pedrarias? Pedrarias was in command, and de Soto had respect for authority. Disobeying Pedrarias would probably have resulted in death. Pedrarias's wife treated de Soto like a son. Most importantly, de Soto had fallen in love with Isabel, Pedrarias's daughter, during the five years that she was in Panama.

Isabel's mother, sensing the attachment between the two, arranged to take her back to Spain. She left in 1520 while de Soto was on an expedition. However, one of Isabel's companions brought de Soto a book with mother-of-pearl binding in which Isabel had written a note: "I will wait for you all of my life, darling." Earlier, Isabel had given him a silver cross that he wore under his armor. De Soto hoped to marry her someday, but he knew he must gain a large fortune before her family would consider him as a suitable husband for her.

YOU CAN FOLLOW DE SOTO'S VOYAGE ON THE MAP ON PAGE 42.

De Soto remained loyal to Pedrarias through many attempts of others to seize power and topple the governor. When Pedrarias died in 1531, de Soto was present at the funeral.

Pedrarias was an important mentor for de Soto, and his family helped de Soto adjust to life in the New World.

Military and business ventures

De Soto traveled in Panama and Nicaragua on military expeditions. He made money through his slave trading. Seeing the value of having the support of others, he entered into a business partnership with his friends, Hernán Ponce de León and Francisco Campañón.

In Nicaragua in 1524, de Soto fought Spaniards who were trying to claim territory rather than acknowledge Pedrarias's authority. He had clearly won a battle against Gil Gonzáles de Avila when Gonzáles called out for peace. Ponce de León did not trust the request and urged de Soto to finish off the defeated forces. However, de Soto did not doubt the word of his opponent and permitted Gonzáles to withdraw and surrender later.

The fighting in Nicaragua took place in some of the beautiful rain forests of the country.

Three hours later, rather than surrender, Gonzáles attacked with added reinforcements. De Soto was taken prisoner and his personal fortune was seized. Three days later, Gonzáles decided to attack elsewhere. He freed de Soto and returned his sword, but de Soto never forgot the taste of defeat.

The three business partners made back their losses through gold mining operations. However, Campañón soon died. Ponce de León and de Soto sent Campañón's share of the money to his mother and reformed the partnership between themselves.

FACTS

Leadership training

During his short life, de Soto had to fight in many different conditions, from tropical rain forests to mountain snow. He also had to finance and equip his own expeditions. During his early travels, he learned important skills that helped him later in life.

South to Peru

Rescuing Pizarro

When Pedrarias died in 1531, de Soto was free to pursue various options. He could live a quieter life in Panama. He could return to Spain, but had he accomplished enough to win Isabel? He could also go south with the expedition that was led by Pizarro to the land of the **Incas** and their reported gold. He discussed this option with his partner, Ponce de León. Ponce de León told him that Francisco Pizarro offered de Soto the post of **lieutenant general,** the second in command. Pizarro returned from Spain with a commission from the king to explore south of Panama.

De Soto outfitted two ships. With 100 men and 50 horses, he headed south to join Pizarro. When he found Pizarro, he discovered that Pizarro's men had suffered and were in bad shape. The land of islands and mountains was not promising, and Pizarro's brother, Hernando, had already been given the post of second in command.

You can follow de Soto's voyage on the map on page 42.

Despite all of this, de Soto stayed. He was with Pizarro as he entered the mainland and began his march to conquer the Incas. From the beginning, the Spaniards met with opposition and fighting from these fierce warriors.

THE SHIPS.

*Many Spanish explorers in the New World sailed in a type of ship called a **caravel**.*

Contact with the Incas

De Soto was key to Pizarro's success. After the fight for the initial landing, de Soto made peace with the local chief who, through interpreters, gave the Spaniards information about the conditions in the Inca **empire.** Yes, the Incas had a lot of gold, but the greatest supply of gold was beyond the mountains. The Inca empire was in a state of civil war, with two brothers fighting for the title of **emperor.** One brother, Atahualpa, had captured the other, Huascar, and kept him prisoner after killing his wives and children before his eyes.

While Pizarro **scouted** the lowlands, de Soto explored the highlands as far as the main highway of the Incas. Although the Incas were friendly at first, eventually the Spaniards encountered a trap and were attacked. They fought back and took the Incas prisoner. In recognition of de Soto's achievements and to soothe his disappointment at the command he had been given, Pizarro awarded de Soto land and command of a town. De Soto was sent ahead to scout out conditions on the way to the town of Cajamarca, where the Inca emperor was staying. An Inca met him and invited the Spaniards to meet the emperor. However, the only way to Cajamarca lay over the mountains. Traveling over the mountains would be a problem for the men because of the high altitude. Also, it would be hard to lead horses through the rough terrain.

An early 17th-century manuscript shows the Inca emperor Huascar being led away in chains.

The Incas and Emperor Atahualpa

First contact with the emperor

The sight that greeted the Spaniards after their long and difficult journey was not reassuring. Row upon row of white tents lined the valley outside the town. These housed the powerful **Inca** army that had won victories for the **emperor.** The small band of Spaniards marched with flags flying into the city, only to find it emptied of inhabitants. At once, Pizarro sent de Soto with fifteen men to contact the Inca emperor.

Thus, de Soto was the first European to approach the emperor. He dressed in full armor and led his band on their horses at a full charge into the Inca camp. Banners flying and trumpets sounding, de Soto rode along the line of Inca soldiers right up to the throne. De Soto extended an invitation from Pizarro to the emperor to visit the Spaniards. The emperor accepted. The Incas, who had never seen horses, looked in amazement at the ones before them. Then de Soto jumped back on his horse and showed off his skill as a horseman. He ended by galloping up to the emperor and stopping suddenly, so close that some of the froth from the animal's mouth landed on the edge of the emperor's cloak.

YOU CAN FOLLOW DE SOTO'S VOYAGE ON THE MAP ON PAGE 42.

De Soto rode his horse right up to the Inca emperor in a show of his horsemanship.

Treatment of the emperor

The 168 Spaniards could not have won a battle on the open field against the Inca soldiers, whose numbers were estimated at 30,000. The Spaniards laid plans for trapping the emperor in the city. De Soto insisted that the emperor not be killed—only taken prisoner—and that he should be given the chance to accept the king of Spain as his ruler. Pizarro agreed and, in protecting the emperor from other Spaniards, was the only Spaniard wounded in the battle. About seven or eight thousand Incas were killed in the battle that captured the Inca emperor.

Atahualpa, the Inca emperor, was worried that he might lose control if his brother was freed from imprisonment. Therefore, he offered a roomful of gold and a roomful of silver as **ransom** for his freedom. Pizarro agreed. However, when the ransom was divided among the soldiers, Pizarro refused to free the emperor. Although de Soto and Pizarro's brother Hernando had befriended the emperor, they were sent away on other missions, and Pizarro had the emperor killed. De Soto was angry that the emperor had been betrayed.

The gold and silver that Atahualpa offered as ransom came in the form of large works of Peruvian art. Most of it was melted into bars.

The division of gold made de Soto a rich man, even though he received less than Francisco or Hernando Pizarro. According to one report, de Soto's share was "far below what his services or talent **merited.**" He could have returned to Spain with wealth and honor, but Pizarro still needed him.

Cuzco, the Inca Capital

Fighting their way to the capital

When de Soto returned, two days after the death of Atahualpa, he asked to be relieved of his duties. Pizarro could not afford to let him go. He had sent his brother Hernando off to Spain with gold for the king. Pizarro offered de Soto the position of second in command and asked him to help the Spaniards get to the **Inca** capital, Cuzco.

Having killed the **emperor,** the Spaniards no longer had the safe passage they had enjoyed when Atahualpa had cleared the roads for the delivery of the **ransom.** De Soto led the way with forty horses, but hundreds of Inca soldiers **ambushed** his band. The conquest might have had a different ending if de Soto had not pulled his horse free from the arms of an enemy and dashed to the top of a nearby hill, followed by his troops.

YOU CAN FOLLOW DE SOTO'S VOYAGE ON THE MAP ON PAGE 42.

When the Spaniards reached Cuzco, de Soto prevented the Incas from burning the city. Pizarro, his troops, and a new emperor—a brother of the one Atahualpa had imprisoned—marched in triumph into the city. The new emperor swore loyalty to the Spanish king, although he later escaped and fought the Spaniards.

The ancient Inca capital of Cuzco was designed in the shape of a puma, an animal holy to the Incas. The fort and temple complex of Sacsahuaman was on the hill that forms the head of the animal. The royal palaces and other government buildings were located around a large plaza at the midsection. The homes of the **noble** families were in the tail.

Governor of Cuzco

This time when the gold and silver was divided, de Soto received a larger share, and he was made governor of Cuzco. He set up the new government, arranged for new buildings, and protected the city from raids by **rebel** Incas.

However, the most difficult task de Soto faced was trying to keep peace between the forces of Pizarro and Pizarro's partner Diego Almagro, who had arrived at Cajamarca and then fought with Pizarro's force in Cuzco. It took all of de Soto's peace-making skills to arrange an agreement between the two. They finally decided to wait for the king of Spain to determine whether Cuzco was in Pizarro's or Almagro's grant of property.

After all of these troubles, de Soto was even more determined to leave Peru. He signed another partnership agreement with Ponce de León, who arrived in Peru to look after de Soto's property. The agreement covered land in Nicaragua and his new possessions in Peru, as well as ships in Panama. Pizarro gave de Soto a gift of gold upon his departure. The gift recognized de Soto's role in coming to Pizarro's rescue at the beginning of his campaign. It also recognized his military and administrative skills.

Don Diego de Almagro, *Pizarro's partner, quarreled with him over claims to territory and gold.*

Return to Spain

Welcome in Spain

When de Soto returned in 1535, he brought fame for his accomplishments as well as a large amount of gold. The day he landed, he wrote to Doña Isabel, Pedrarias's widow, and asked to be allowed to visit her and her daughter, Isabel. De Soto bought a house and a new wardrobe. Ordinary people, proud of their hero, stood in the streets and the city squares just to watch him pass.

Isabel, now almost thirty, had waited for him. De Soto brought expensive gifts—a gold **Inca** collar for Isabel, pearl pendants for her mother, and an emerald from the **emperor's ransom** for the widow's brother-in-law.

De Soto also visited his family in Extremadura. His father had died, but his mother was proud of her second son's achievements. His town of Jerez was now calling itself a city, with an official **charter** from the Spanish emperor.

The wedding with Isabel was finally set for November of 1536. De Soto spent time courting Isabel and furnishing their home. These were happy days for him. As part of her **dowry,** Isabel gave her husband valuable land in Panama that had been the home of Pedrarias, as well as some cattle. In turn, he gave Isabel a large sum of money.

This 16th-century painting shows how a wealthy woman like Isabel might have dressed.

Married life

The newlyweds seemed very happy in their new home in Seville, where they entertained a constant stream of relatives. De Soto kept in touch with developments in the New World through news reaching Spain. He had been awarded the highest honor of knight, the Order of Santiago. He met Emperor Charles and even lent him some money.

This portrait shows the Emperor Charles of Spain at the age of 48.

De Soto and his companions from the New World were in great demand in Spain. In taverns and inns and other meeting places, people begged to hear stories of their travels. At a relatively young age, de Soto was rich, famous, and happily married. He could have lived out the rest of his life comfortably in Spain.

Still, de Soto wanted action, and he hoped to show his wife their property in the New World. In 1537, he asked permission to conquer Ecuador, with rights to the Amazon River basin. Instead, the emperor asked him to conquer what is now Florida. He made de Soto governor of Cuba, even though he had never been there. This time, de Soto would lead his own expedition instead of being second in command. Others, including Juan Ponce de León, had gone to Florida before him and met with hostility from the local tribes. But who knew what he would find in this largely unexplored territory? No one even knew the size of this territory—the maps of the day were still incomplete.

The New Expedition

YOU CAN FOLLOW DE SOTO'S VOYAGE ON THE MAP ON PAGE 43.

Organizing the force

De Soto was given a year to recruit and equip a force to go to the New World. With his

Sailors in the 16th century thought sea serpents, mermaids, and other imaginary creatures lived beyond the boundaries of the known world.

fame and wealth, he was able to attract thousands of men. He selected the youngest, strongest, and most loyal. The king showed his favor by granting titles and land in the territory of Florida. However, as usual in such voyages, the leader had to finance the expedition. De Soto used most of his wealth to outfit the ships.

By now, **plunder** and the slave trade were no longer allowed as a way of financing the fighting force. Charles and his wife, Empress Isabel of Portugal, wanted settlers to hold the land. Workers were needed, and volunteers who brought their wives and children with them were given free passage. With increasing numbers of Spanish **colonists,** it was now somewhat safer to live in the New World. Spreading the Roman Catholic faith was also an important motivation for these expeditions. Settlers still suffered the hardships of building a new home, starting over, and facing Indian **revolts.**

When de Soto boarded his **flagship,** Isabel went with him. At the last minute, de Soto received news that his mother had died in far away Jerez. He did not let that stop him. He set sail on April 6, 1538, with his fleet of thirty ships and the best-equipped expedition ever to leave for the New World.

Shores of the New World

The journey across the ocean went smoothly until they reached the shores of Cuba. The settlers there had been threatened by pirates and mistook de Soto's ships for another attack. They sent out a rider to call bad instructions to the pilots of the ships. De Soto's ship struck a reef. However, when they realized who it was, the inhabitants welcomed the new governor and gave him gifts.

De Soto made his headquarters at Santiago and began training his men. He had brought 200 horses from Spain and added an additional 200 from the island. He ordered the rebuilding of Havana, which had been attacked by French pirates. He sent out two ships to **scout** the coast of Florida, make maps, and return with natives to serve as interpreters.

Hernán Ponce de León, de Soto's old partner, landed in Cuba, but he was obviously trying to hide the true wealth of their partnership from de Soto. He overlooked Ponce de León's **treachery** in order to maintain their friendship.

Ponce de León said he would contribute 10,000 **pesos** for the expedition. Later, he asked Isabel for the money to be returned to him, but she refused and told him he would go to jail if he did not comply with his promise. Isabel was a strong woman, and de Soto left her in charge as governor of Cuba when he left for Florida on May 18, 1539.

Havana, Cuba had one of the best ports in the West Indies, with an easily defended narrow entrance.

Prior explorers

De Soto was not the first European to set foot in Florida. That honor had gone to Juan Ponce de León in 1513. In 1493, Ponce de León had been with Christopher Columbus on his second trip to the New World. Later, he gained permission to seek out new lands and slaves, though he had also heard tales of a magical spring called the **Fountain of Youth.** In Florida he encountered hostility from the native people. On his second trip to the west coast, an arrow wounded Ponce de León and he died.

YOU CAN FOLLOW DE SOTO'S VOYAGE ON THE MAP ON PAGE 43.

Traders followed Ponce de León's trip. In 1519, Alvarez de Pineda was sent to map the shores of Florida. He discovered that it was a peninsula—not an island. However, it was Panfilo de Narvaez's treatment of the Native Americans in 1527 that caused de Soto the most trouble in 1539. The trader had cut off the nose of the local chief, Hirrihigua, and thrown the chief's mother to the Spaniards' attack dogs. Narvaez sent his ships away in order to go overland to look for a city that had gold. He lost hundreds of men; only four survived. But his mistreatment of the Native Americans caused them to look on all Spaniards as enemies. It took courage for men to follow de Soto into this land.

*Dogs were often used by the Spaniards as weapons against the Native Americans. **Missionary** priests sometimes tried to protect them, but they were not always successful.*

A cold welcome

The first attack on de Soto's men came at 3:00 A.M., the day after they first left their ships. The sound of a trumpet calling to the ship for reinforcements, along with the superior weapons of the Spaniards, caused the Native Americans to retreat. De Soto ordered the rest of the 350 horses to be brought ashore so that they could regain their strength after being stabled on the ships. Then he pushed north.

The first city they came to was Ocita. Here, they met Chief Hirrihigua, the man who hated Spaniards because of what the Spanish trader Narvaez had done to him. De Soto sent an invitation to the chief explaining that, just as with other people, there were good Spaniards and bad Spaniards. However, Hirrihigua refused.

De Soto's Indian guides told him about a rumor of a white man from Narvaez's expedition who was living under the protection of a chief named Mococo. De Soto sent one of his captains, Baltasar Gallegos, with troops to find the Spaniard. The troops galloped toward a group of Indians with red paint, shaved skulls with one tuft, feathers, and **loincloths.** One of the tribesmen called out: "Seville! Seville! In the name of God and the Blessed Virgin do not kill me. I am a Christian." They had found Juan Ortiz.

DE SOTO LANDING HIS FORCES IN FLORIDA.

De Soto and his officers supervise the landing in Florida in 1539. The horse, which is not native to the New World, was one of the Spaniards' most valuable weapons.

Juan Ortiz

Captured!

Juan Ortiz had been a young soldier on one of Narvaez's ships. Wanting revenge, Chief Hirrihigua had tricked the Spaniards into sending four soldiers ashore for a feast while four of his men went on board the ship. The Spaniards were suspicious, but sent four men ashore to **scout** the situation. Hirrihigua's men swam ashore, and the four Spaniards were taken prisoner. However, instead of trying to rescue the four men, Narvaez sailed away and left them behind.

YOU CAN FOLLOW DE SOTO'S VOYAGE ON THE MAP ON PAGE 43.

One by one, the Spanish prisoners were forced to run between rows of warriors shooting arrows at them. The warriors were trying to torture them, but not kill them. Eventually, three of the Spaniards died, but the chief's wife and daughters begged him to let them keep Ortiz as a slave. The chief agreed, but often tortured Ortiz by having arrows shot at him. Once, the chief started to roast Ortiz over a fire. Ortiz was badly burned but was nursed back to health by the chief's women, who again pleaded for his life. Finally, when the chief decided to kill Ortiz, the women arranged to send him to a relative and friend, Chief Mococo.

The Timucuan Indians of Florida were fine archers who would tip their arrows with flaming moss when attacking a village.

In disguise

Fortunately for Ortiz, Chief Mococo, who was engaged to marry one of these women, agreed to give him protection. The chief assigned a couple to show Ortiz how to live and how to fight. Ortiz was tattooed and dressed like the other men. He became Mococo's personal servant.

Ortiz had lived two years with Hirrihigua and ten years with Mococo. What hope did he have of ever seeing Spain again? However, when news of de Soto's expedition reached Mococo, the chief decided to send Ortiz to de Soto in return for de Soto's protection.

Gallegos, the captain who had found Ortiz, immediately sent word to Mococo and invited him to meet with de Soto. Mococo, who was then about 30 years old, pledged friendship with de Soto. Mococo's mother was not so trusting and came to the camp to offer herself as a hostage in place of her son, whom she thought was being held against his will. De Soto treated the mother with courtesy and presented her with gifts.

Timucuan warriors were tattooed. Their bows were as tall as they were. Scholars cannot decide whether they wore basket hats or had elaborate hairdos.

About this time, another woman made news in the Spaniard's camp. Among the thousands of soldiers was a woman, Francisca Hinestrosa, who had disguised herself as a man so she could travel with her husband. De Soto had banned women from following the soldiers. However, she was pardoned and became valuable as a nurse to the wounded. Meanwhile Ortiz, with his knowledge of the local tribal life and language, became a valued member of the de Soto expedition and wrote an account of it.

27

Travels North

Hostile territory

On June 15, de Soto moved north and left a small force at Ocita, along with two ships. A group of **scouts** led the way. De Soto traveled in the center, surrounded by his guards. The artillery and the people in charge of supplies brought up the rear. The expedition had brought a huge supply of pigs to provide food. The land that they entered was often swampy and dangerous, and in several places they had to build bridges.

If the land was hard, the reception from the local tribes was even worse. Though de Soto tried to offer gifts and friendship, the tribal chiefs had encountered enough trouble from other Spaniards. They ordered de Soto's men away. Near Ocala, the chief of the Timucuans tried an **ambush** of de Soto's forces. Near what is now Gainesville, Chief Vitacucho tried to lead the Spaniards into a trap. Ortiz overheard the plot and warned de Soto of the danger, so he was prepared. In battle, de Soto's horse was killed by eight arrows. A soldier lent him another horse, and de Soto went on to defeat the native warriors.

Moving north again, they crossed the Suwannee River. They came to the 250-house center of the Apalachee tribes, which is now the city of Tallahassee. De Soto decided to spend the winter at Apalachicola Bay.

YOU CAN FOLLOW DE SOTO'S VOYAGE ON THE MAP ON PAGE 43.

This coin, minted between 1505 and 1517, was found in Tallahassee, Florida, at de Soto's first winter camp.

The Spaniards were impressed with the beauty of this chief.

Peace

On March 3, 1540, de Soto moved northeast into what is now Georgia. The chief of the Cofas was friendly. De Soto decided that the cannon he had brought was more trouble than it was worth. So after demonstrating its power, he made a gift of this "Channel of Thunder" to the chief. In return, he received a loan of 700 men to carry the expedition's supplies to the kingdom of Cofitachequi.

They headed north again and crossed rivers and a desert. By May 1, they had crossed the Savannah River to land around what is now Augusta, Georgia. Six warriors and a young girl appeared and asked whether they had come in peace. Because the Spaniards had come in peace, she and the warriors crossed the river. Several hours later, more canoes arrived. The warriors carried another young girl on a litter. She was dressed in fine white cotton and had a headdress of eagle feathers. She reported that her people had suffered from sickness and poor crops, but she offered to share food and housing with the Spaniards. She gave de Soto a beautiful pearl necklace. In return, de Soto gave her his ruby and gold ring. These were members of the Creek tribe, who had great stores of pearls that they offered to the Spaniards.

Battles

Over the Appalachians

De Soto and his men headed north, into what is now South Carolina. With help from friendly tribes, they negotiated the **gorge** of the Hiwassee River, near present-day Murphy, North Carolina. They came out on the highlands of the Tennessee River and passed the place where Chattanooga would later be founded. Three weeks later, they became the first Europeans to cross the Appalachian Mountains, a distance of 150 miles (249 kilometers). De Soto secured more people to carry supplies by holding the area chiefs captive.

YOU CAN FOLLOW DE SOTO'S VOYAGE ON THE MAP ON PAGE 43.

The expedition entered the territory of the Choctaw in the fall of 1540. Chief Tascaluza met de Soto and offered him carriers for his forces when they reached the town of Mauvilla, north of what is now Mobile, Alabama. De Soto's **scouts** warned him of an **ambush** because of the efforts to strengthen the town's defenses. However, when the chief sent a gift of bread made from chestnuts, de Soto decided to enter the town to show bravery.

During the entertainment, the chief excused himself to talk with someone and snubbed de Soto. In response, a Spaniard struck a Choctaw, and Indian warriors poured out of their hiding places, yelling and shooting arrows. The Spaniards fled quickly, leaving some of their belongings behind.

A highway through the Great Smoky Mountains follows the same trail used by de Soto and his army.

Fighting and losses

With the arrival of reinforcements, de Soto organized them into four groups to attack the four sides of the fortress. One soldier carried a torch to set fire to the roofs of the houses. De Soto's battle plan was successful, but the Indians fought fiercely. Some even hanged themselves instead of surrendering.

De Soto led the charge into the main plaza of the fort. However, as he was standing in his stirrups, an arrow found its way past the armor and struck him in the bottom. For the next five hours of fighting, de Soto could not sit back down in his saddle.

The **casualties** were high. Almost 2,500 Native Americans died. Though they won, the Spaniards lost 22 men, including de Soto's nephew and his brother-in-law. Between 150 and 250 of the Spaniards were injured. Eighty horses were dead or injured. Most of the Spaniards' possessions, including valuable pearls, were burned. Since the beginning of the land expedition, 102 Spaniards had died. Many of the men were becoming discouraged, and some officers planned to **mutiny.** Though de Soto had received reports that his ships were waiting for him on the coast, he knew that if he returned now, he would not be able to come back again. He turned away from his ships and set a course to the north to find a place to spend the winter.

The bloodiest battle between Spaniards and Native Americans occurred here at Mauvilla.

31

The Mississippi River

The road ahead

De Soto had no way of knowing what lay ahead. He and his force spent the winter in the Chickasaw territory in what is now northeastern Mississippi. One night, when the **sentries** were not paying attention, a group of warriors attacked. They might have wiped out the Spaniards, but luckily their flaming arrows panicked the horses and made the Chickasaw fear a **cavalry** charge. They withdrew. About one dozen Spaniards were killed, including the only woman, Francisca Hinestrosa, who had cared for the sick. They lost even more of their supplies and about three-quarters of their hogs. The Chickasaw later tried another attack, but this time the sentries gave warning and they were defeated.

You CAN FOLLOW DE SOTO'S VOYAGE ON THE MAP ON PAGE 43.

On April 26, 1541, the Spaniards moved on through a country of plains and small villages. They came upon a fort of the Muskhogee tribe, who dressed and spoke differently than the tribes they had already met. They captured the fort, but the Spaniards were suffering from lack of food and salt.

They came to a village called Quizquiz, where the chief gave them food and told them about a great river to the north. After a march of four days, on May 8, 1541, de Soto came within sight of the great Mississippi River.

De Soto is credited as being the first European explorer to see the Mississippi River, which he called the "Rio Grande."

Crossing the river

De Soto knelt and thanked God for allowing him to make such a great discovery. The priests offered prayers. The Spaniards were impressed with this great river. They called it the Rio Grande, even though the Native Americans had already named it Mississippi. Because of the spring floods, the river was nearly two miles (3.2 kilometers) across. The Spaniards had no way of knowing that they were seeing the third-longest river in the world. Other explorers had investigated the river at its mouth, but historians credit de Soto as being the first European discoverer.

Now the Spaniards began to build four rafts with sails and oars on which to cross the river. It took almost one month before they had cut down trees and built the rafts necessary to carry the expedition across to the other side. Then de Soto gave the order for the rafts to be dismantled and the nails and hardware kept for future use. The crossing was probably made near what is now Sunflower Landing, Mississippi.

The Spaniards crossed the Mississippi on June 18, 1541.

FACTS

The Mississippi River
The longest river in North America, the Mississippi is 2,350 miles (3,187 kilometers) long. With the rivers that flow into it, it drains an area of 1,200,000 square miles (3,108,000 square kilometers), one-eighth of the area of North America.

Arkansas and Louisiana

Mixed welcomes

De Soto turned north along the banks of the river. Five days later, he came to Casqui, which was inhabited by the Kaskaskis tribe, who had suffered a great **drought.** The Kaskaskis told the Spaniards that just as the Spanish weapons were better, so their religion must be. They asked the Spaniards to pray for rain. De Soto put a pinewood cross on a hill. The priests blessed the cross, and the thousands of Kaskaskis who had gathered for the ceremony tried to follow the kneeling and rising of the Spaniards. The following day, rain drenched the fields.

The Spaniards rested here for six days and obtained new clothing from the Kaskaskis's animal hides. When the Spaniards moved on, they found Indians living in tepees. They also saw bison. They discovered no gold, but did find copper and salt. De Soto turned his forces west and hoped to find the fabulous cities or the sea that had been reported by other Spanish explorers.

They ran into another kind of welcome from the Caddo tribe in Tula. When the Spaniards arrived, the men and women of the tribe fought them for hours and then attacked later at night, before they were defeated and peace was made. The Spaniards considered them the best fighters they had met.

YOU CAN FOLLOW DE SOTO'S VOYAGE ON THE MAP ON PAGE 43.

No European had ever seen a bison before de Soto and his men arrived in the New World.

34

Winter and plans for return

With winter coming, de Soto needed to find a place for his troops. He was advised to go to Autianque, where he would find housing and food. He planned to winter here beginning on November 21, 1541. The local chief brought gifts, but the chief of the region had **scouts** observing the Spaniards. De Soto had his men build a fence around their quarters. He ordered the men to attend to their weapons and staged some mock attacks to keep the soldiers alert. They also had parties and guitar playing. The plans at the end of their winter stay were to return to the Mississippi River to make boats and return to Cuba before making settlements. His force of effective fighters was probably down to around 300 men and 40 horses—mostly lame because of lack of iron for shoes. However, many hundreds of Native Americans had joined him. During this winter, Juan Ortiz died, which deprived de Soto of his most effective interpreter.

The expedition took a more southerly route, through Arkansas, than the one by which they had come. They rested at the village of Anilco and then pressed on through forests and swamps with alligators and **malaria**-carrying insects. They came to central Louisiana and stayed at the town of Guachoya, which many historians believe is near the Mississippi River and today's town of Ferriday.

De Soto planned to spend the winter in what is now northeastern Mississippi.

Death of De Soto

Guachoya

The local chief brought fruit and fish for food and animal skins for clothing. He also asked the Spaniards to help in a raid against an enemy chief, Quigaltam, across the river. De Soto had come down with a fever and was too sick to go, but he sent troops to assist the Guachoya and punish Quigaltam for his rude reply to the offer of friendship that the Spaniards had sent. More than one hundred of the enemy men were killed, and women and children were imprisoned. The Guachoya **plundered** the houses of their enemies and even took the bones of the ancient chiefs from the graves to scatter them.

In spite of his illness, de Soto tried to maintain discipline among his forces. The boats that he had ordered built were under construction. Then de Soto's illness—perhaps **malaria** or **dysentery**—worsened.

You can follow de Soto's voyage on the map on page 43.

His fever rose and he realized that he was near death. He received the **sacraments** from his cousin, Friar Luis. Then he assembled his officers, thanked them for their loyalty, and named his **successor,** Luis Moscoso. On May 21, 1542, de Soto died. He was in his early forties.

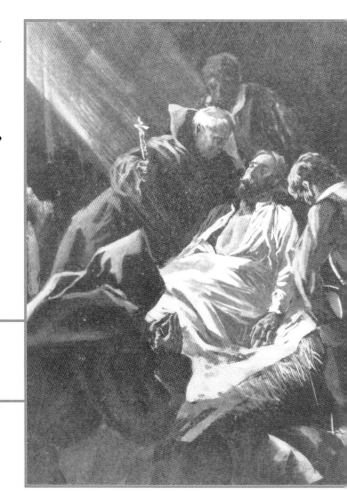

De Soto had survived many military attacks but died from illness.

The Mississippi River became de Soto's final resting place. However, most sources say he was placed in the water in a log coffin, not wrapped in cloth.

Burial

Moscoso and the other officers had kept de Soto's illness a secret from the Native Americans, even though the local chief kept asking about him. They buried de Soto's body at night. The next day, the Spaniards made a big show of activity to fool the Guachoya into thinking that their leader was better and was giving many orders. However, the tighter security around de Soto's quarters and the grief on peoples' faces gave away the secret. Also, they did not believe the explanation given—that he had gone to visit his father, the Sun.

When the Spaniards were ready to leave Guachoya, they faced a difficult decision. They had seen how the local chief and his warriors had torn up the graves of their enemies. They feared the same thing would happen to de Soto's grave when they left. They decided that it would be better if de Soto's body was buried in the Mississippi River. Some of the officers went fishing to discover a deep place in the river. Because they had no stones to use to weigh down the body, they hollowed out the bottom of a heavy oak tree. Then they dug up the body, placed it in this coffin, and nailed on a lid. Then his officers, a priest, and his relatives lowered the tree into the great river.

The Survivors

The expedition

De Soto's plan had been to build boats, return to Cuba, and then return with settlers. However, many of the men thought that it would be just a short distance to Mexico, called New Spain, in the west. Moscoso and his men marched west and crossed the Red River near present day Shreveport and, turning southwest, went as far as Bryan, north of Houston, Texas. It was now October. Food and supplies were low. The land would not meet their needs. Moscoso and the others decided to return to Guachoya for the winter.

The Spaniards were able to build seven boats, with sails made of leather and cloaks. They made water barrels and cables, and created anchors from their stirrups. Local tribes contributed ropes and corn. They continued their work during the spring floods. During a period of high water in June, they floated their ships to the river.

You can follow De Soto's voyage on the map on page 43.

In July of 1543, the Spaniards began their journey down the river, still subject to Indian attacks. They kept close to the coastline of the Gulf of Mexico and made it to a Spanish settlement in Panuco about September, 1543. The survivors finally reached Mexico City, where they disbanded. Some returned to Spain, and others remained in Mexico or went to war in Peru.

The Spaniards were the superior fighting force on land, but the Native Americans had the advantage in a fight on the water.

De Soto's will

In his **will,** de Soto **reaffirmed** his Roman Catholic faith. He and Isabel had no children of their own, but he remembered his brother and several other family members. He honored his partnership agreement with Hernan Ponce de León and left him half his goods. Other gifts included substantial sums that went to Isabel.

De Soto's wife Isabel was heartbroken to hear of her husband's death and burial in the Mississippi River.

Isabel had been sending ships with supplies out to him each summer. Diego Maldonado and Gomez Arias, the captains, had explored the coasts seeking news of de Soto, but they were unsuccessful. In 1543, they sailed along the Atlantic coast of Florida up to Cape Cod in Massachusetts. On their way back, they stopped at Veracruz in the Gulf before returning to Havana, Cuba. Thus, they brought to Isabel late that year the news that her husband had died. She followed the instructions in de Soto's will and, heartbroken, died a short time later.

De Soto's Legacy

Personal achievements

The second son of a poor but **noble** Spanish family, de Soto had to make his own way in the world. He became a recognized hero of Spain. De Soto's service to the Pedrarias family showed his loyalty and trustworthiness. His service in the New World advanced the interests of his king. If he had not been present to help Pizarro, the Spaniards may well have been defeated in Peru. He risked his life but won a fortune in gold and fame as a fighter.

De Soto married Isabel, his childhood sweetheart. She had waited for him for years and helped him in securing his wish to get the king's approval for an expedition that he would lead. He organized that expedition in a thorough manner and led the exploration of lands where no Europeans had gone before. They crossed the Appalachian mountains and the Mississippi River, covering about 2,175 miles (3,500 kilometers) in all. In his lifetime, Hernando de Soto had discovered more territory traveling over land routes than any other explorer of his day.

Archaeological digs in the southeastern part of the United States have provided evidence of the Spaniards' presence in the New World.

His place in history

Historians who write about de Soto portray him as either a daring, bold, and talented adventurer, or as a cruel killer of Native Americans and their cultures. He was both. He lived at a time when there was much cruelty, both in Europe and among the Native American tribes. There was also cruelty between the Europeans and the Native Americans.

Was de Soto right to try to conquer the New World in the name of his king and his church? The question probably would not have occurred to him. After all, the **Moors** had conquered much of Spain and had been pushed out just before the time of his birth. He would have seen conquest for Spain as an honorable service.

Was the expedition he led worth the loss of life, both Spanish and Native American? No gold was found. Would an **empire** of what is now Florida, Georgia, South Carolina, North Carolina, Tennessee, Alabama, Mississippi, Arkansas, and Louisiana be worth the struggle? Garcilaso de la Vega, a sixteenth-century writer, reported on de Soto's North American expedition. He gave this answer in 1599 about de Soto's effort: "If he had lived two years longer, he would have repaired the damage done in the past, with the help of reinforcements he would have requested and received, via the Mighty River, as he had planned. This could have been the start of an empire that today could have competed with New Spain and Peru."

In his early travels, Hernando de Soto covered an amazing amount of land. He lived in Panama until Pedrarias's death in 1531.

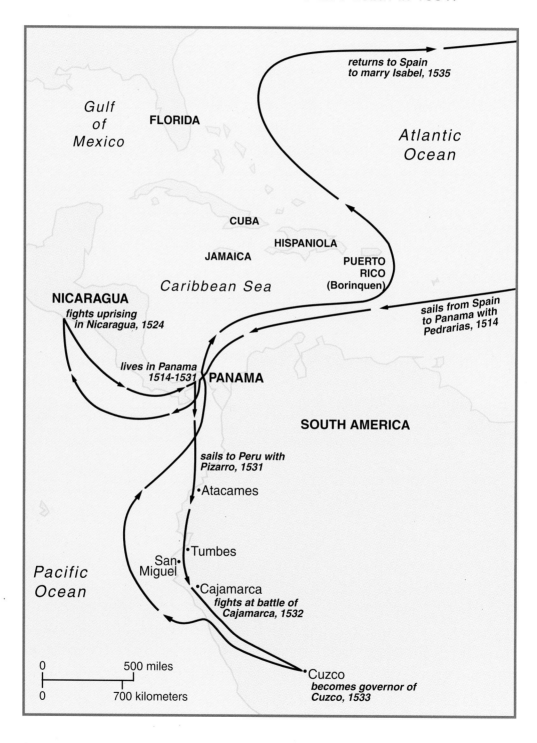

Gulf of Mexico

FLORIDA

Atlantic Ocean

returns to Spain to marry Isabel, 1535

CUBA

HISPANIOLA

JAMAICA

PUERTO RICO (Borinquen)

Caribbean Sea

sails from Spain to Panama with Pedrarias, 1514

NICARAGUA

fights uprising in Nicaragua, 1524

lives in Panama 1514-1531

PANAMA

SOUTH AMERICA

sails to Peru with Pizarro, 1531

•Atacames

•Tumbes

San• Miguel

Pacific Ocean

•Cajamarca

fights at battle of Cajamarca, 1532

| 0 | 500 miles |
| 0 | 700 kilometers |

•Cuzco

becomes governor of Cuzco, 1533

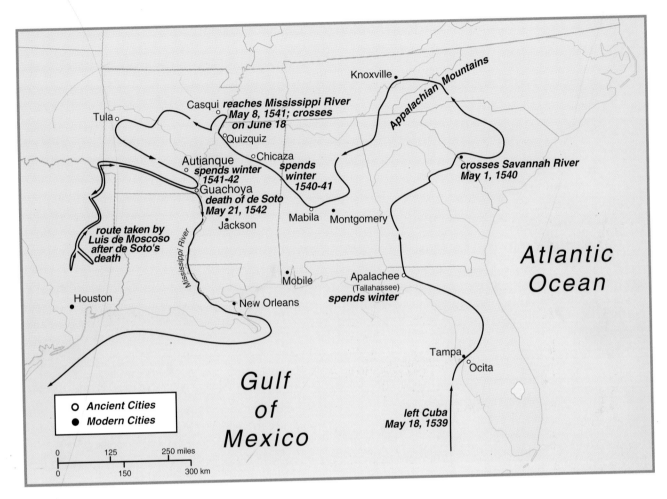

De Soto returned to the New World from Spain in 1538 with 30 ships. His expedition landed in Cuba, where he was attacked by Spanish settlers who mistook de Soto and his men for pirates. After clearing up the mistake, de Soto spent the winter in Cuba, training his men. On May 18, 1539, he set sail for Florida. No one is sure of the exact route he took through the southeastern United States, but historians have been able to piece much of it together from journals and accounts written by de Soto and his men. The route shown above is generally agreed upon by historians, although there are some that disagree.

Timeline

1469	The marriage of Isabella of Castile and Ferdinand of Aragon brings together two powerful Spanish territories.
1492	Columbus reaches the New World.
1496–1501	Estimated birthdate of Hernando de Soto.
1513	Juan Ponce de León discovers Florida; Vasco Nuñéz de Balboa crosses Panama and discovers the Pacific Ocean.
1514?	De Soto sails to the New World with Pedrarias.
1516	Charles I becomes king of Spain.
1519	De Soto fights in western Panama and is promoted to captain.
	Charles I of Spain becomes Charles V, Holy Roman Emperor.
	Balboa is beheaded.
	Alvarez de Pineda discovers that Florida is not an island.
1520	Pedrarias's daughter, Isabel de Bobadilla, leaves Panama for Spain.
1524	De Soto helps to conquer Nicaragua and engages in business there.
1531	Pedrarias dies at the age of 90.
	De Soto sails for Peru to help Francisco Pizarro conquer the **Incas.**
1532	De Soto fights at the battle of Cajamarca, during which the Inca emperor is captured.
1533	The Spaniards execute the Inca emperor and capture the Inca capital, Cuzco.
1534	Pizarro names de Soto lieutenant governor of Cuzco.
1535	De Soto, now a rich man, leaves Peru for Spain.
1536	De Soto marries Isabel de Bobadilla.
1537	Charles V grants de Soto the right to conquer Florida, naming him governor-general of that territory and also governor of Cuba.
1538	De Soto's expedition leaves Spain for Cuba. De Soto organizes the government of Cuba and prepares for an expedition to Florida.

1539	De Soto lands in Florida, marches north, and winters at Apalachicola Bay.
1540	De Soto marches over the Appalachians, has losses in the battle at Mauvilla, and winters in Mississippi.
1541	De Soto reaches the Mississippi River on May 8, explores into Arkansas, and winters in Guachoya in Louisiana.
1542	De Soto dies of illness on May 21 and is buried in the Mississippi River. Luis Moscoso takes over leadership of the expedition and tries to reach Mexico through Texas, but returns to Guachoya for winter.
1543	Moscoso escapes down the Mississippi River and along the Gulf coast to a Spanish settlement. Isabel receives word of her husband's death and returns to Spain.
1556	Charles I of Spain dies.

More Books to Read

Chrisman, Abbott. *Hernando de Soto.* Austin, Tex.: Raintree Steck-Vaughn Publishers, 1991.

Morley, Jacqueline. *Exploring North America.* Lincolnwood, Ill.: NTC Contemporary Publishing Co., 1996.

Sanchez, Richard. *Spain: Explorers and Conquerors.* Minneapolis, Minn.: ABDO Publishing Company, 1994.

Tames, Richard. *Great Explorers.* Danbury, Conn.: Franklin Watts, Inc., 1997.

Glossary

ambush hidden place from which a surprise attack can be made, or to attack in such a way

casualty person or thing injured, lost, or destroyed

caravel small ship with three or four masts used in the fifteenth and sixteenth centuries

cavalry soldiers mounted on horseback

charter official document listing the rights and duties of the people or place to whom it is given

colonist person sent out by a state to settle a new territory

conquistador leader in the Spanish conquest of the Americas during the fifteenth and sixteenth centuries

court a ruler's assembly of advisers and officers

don honorary title similar to "sir" in English

dowry property a woman brings to her husband in marriage

drought long period of time with very little rainfall

dysentery serious disease with symptoms that include severe diarrhea

emperor ruler of an empire

empire group of territories or peoples under one ruler

fencing art of fighting with swords

flagship ship that carries the commander of a group of ships and flies his flag

Fountain of Youth magical fountain, believed to exist in the New World, that would make a person young again

gorge narrow passage through land, often a steep-sided canyon

Incas Native American people of Peru who had a highly developed civilization when the Spaniards came

Knights Templar order of Christian knights that fought in holy wars

lance weapon with a long handle and a sharp steel head, used by soldiers on horseback

lieutenant general second in command

loincloth cloth that covers the area between the waist and the thighs

malaria disease spread by mosquitoes with symptoms that include chills and fever

merit deserve

missionary someone who travels to another country to spread their religion

Moors Muslims from northern Africa who conquered Spain in the eighth century

mutiny to refuse, as a group, to obey authority

noble of high birth or rank, or a person of high rank

page in the Middle Ages, a boy in training to become a knight

peso unit of Spanish currency

plunder to rob or steal openly and by force, as during war

pope leader of the Roman Catholic church

ransom money paid to free a person from captivity or punishment

reaffirm to declare again dedication to someone or something

rebel person who refuses to give in to authority

revolt open fight against the government

sacrament religious ceremony that is especially sacred, such as the last rites before death

scout to explore an area to obtain information, or someone who goes on such a mission

sentry person on duty as a guard

successor person who is next in line for a throne, title, or office

treachery act of betraying trust

will legal document that states who will receive a person's possessions after their death

Index